LEADING WOMEN

Taylor Swift

Pop Music
Superstar

KELLY SPENCE

Cavendish
Square

New York

W

J
921
SWIFT, T

Published in 2017 by Cavendish Square Publishing, LLC
243 5th Avenue, Suite 136, New York, NY 10016

Library of Congress Cataloging-in-Publication Data

Names: Spence, Kelly.
Title: Taylor Swift : pop music superstar / Kelly Spence.
Description: New York : Cavendish Square Publishing, 2016. | Series: Leading women | Includes bibliographical references and index.
Identifiers: LCCN 2016004975 (print) | LCCN 2016005302 (ebook) | ISBN 9781502619914 (library bound) | ISBN 9781502619921 (ebook)
Subjects: LCSH: Swift, Taylor, 1989---Juvenile literature. | Women country musicians--United States--Biography--Juvenile literature. | Country musicians--United States--Biography--Juvenile literature.
Classification: LCC ML3930.S989 S62 2016 (print) | LCC ML3930.S989 (ebook) | DDC 782.421642092--dc23
LC record available at http://lccn.loc.gov/2016004975

Editorial Director: David McNamara
Editor: Elizabeth Schmermund
Copy Editor: Rebecca Rohan
Art Director: Jeffrey Talbot
Designer: Stephanie Flecha
Production Assistant: Karol Szymczuk
Photo Research: J8 Media

Printed in the United States of America

CONTENTS

CHAPTER ONE

Little Girl, Big Dreams

P op superstar, celebrity entrepreneur, and role model to millions—Taylor Swift is one of the biggest names in music today. Through her rise to the top, Swift has gained an army of followers from around the world. Her down-to-earth attitude, quirky sense of humor, and generous spirit allow her to connect with her fans. The relatable stories she shares through her music and lyrics resonate with people, particularly young girls who have grown up alongside the singer-songwriter. Each of Swift's five albums reads like an autobiography, documenting the pop star's ascent from a sixteen-year-old chasing dreams of stardom to arguably the most popular artist on the music scene today.

Taylor Swift's childhood home in Pennsylvania.

This singer-songwriter has certainly come a long way in over a decade spent in the public eye. But long before her millions of fans (called Swifties), record-breaking singles, and countless awards, Swift was a just a little girl with big dreams.

The Story Begins

Swift's parents, Andrea Garner and Scott Kingsley Swift, met during the 1980s in Houston, Texas. Both Andrea and Scott had built successful careers in the financial industry. Scott was a financial advisor for Merrill Lynch, and Andrea was a financial marketing executive. After the couple tied the knot down south in 1988, they headed north to Pennsylvania to put down roots. Andrea and Scott settled in Reading, Pennsylvania, a midsize city located just over one hour northwest of Philadelphia.

In the final weeks of 1989, the couple marked a new chapter with the arrival of their first child. Taylor Alison Swift was born during the early morning hours of December 13, 1989. Andrea and Scott named their new baby girl after legendary folk singer James Taylor. Andrea, a seasoned business professional, also liked the gender-neutral name, believing it could give her daughter a leg up in the future when searching for jobs. Swift explained in an interview with *Rolling Stone*: "My mom thought it was cool that if you got a business card that said 'Taylor,' you wouldn't know if it was a guy or a girl. She wanted me to be a business person in a business world." (Swift is living out that dream; she is often recognized for her keen head for business in navigating the music industry.) It was clear from the start they had a special little girl on their hands; just hours after Swift was born, Andrea remembers the pediatrician noting that she was a sweet baby, but she knew exactly what she wanted and how to get it.

The proud new parents brought Swift home to the family farm in nearby Wyomissing, a suburb of Reading. Andrea and Scott wanted to give their family a country upbringing, taking on farming as a hobby. As a side business, the Swifts grew Christmas trees for the holiday season. Two years later, the family grew again with the arrival of Swift's little brother, Austin. Soon, Andrea left her job to become a full-time mom to Taylor and Austin. Alongside Christmas trees, the farm was home to seven horses. In true cowgirl fashion, Swift rode and competed in horseback-riding competitions for much of her childhood. While their children were too young to help with most of the work on the farm, Andrea and Scott gave their daughter the important task of removing praying mantis pods from the trees.

Stories and Songs

With acres of property to explore, Swift's creative juices starting flowing early. She spent many days roaming around the farm and was able to let her imagination run wild.

For Swift, words offered a magical world where anything was possible. In an interview with Katie Couric, she explains her early fascination with stories: "I think I fell in love with words before I fell in love with music. All I wanted to do was talk. And all I wanted to do was hear stories." As a little girl, Swift would change the words to nursery rhymes, listing Dr. Seuss and Shel Silverstein as some of her favorite writers. In elementary school, she discovered a love and talent for writing poetry. In the fourth grade, she won a national poetry contest for her poem "Monster in My Closet." As a winning entry, the poem was published as part of a children's poetry collection. The expressiveness of poetry provided a natural transition into songwriting for the ambitious young dreamer. During one trip to the shore when she was eleven, Swift spent an entire summer penning a 350-page novel, *A Girl Named Girl*.

Paired with young Swift's early love of words was a love of music. Swift's musical education started early. During her pregnancy, Andrea rocked out to the British band Def Leppard. Musical talent also ran in Swift's blood. Andrea's mother, Marjorie Finlay, had been a famous opera singer. She was one of the first people to ignite Swift's dream of stardom.

Stage fright was never a problem for Swift and, from an early age, she loved to perform. The family had purchased a beach house in Stone Harbor along the New Jersey shore when Swift was two. During summer visits to the beach, as a solo act, Swift would roam from blanket to blanket, performing songs for strangers. She favored Disney tunes, particularly those from *The Lion King*. Her parents noticed their daughter could quickly learn the words to many songs. Swift would come out of the movie theater singing the tracks to the latest Disney movie after only seeing it once.

Country Style

At six, Swift fell in love with country after receiving a Christmas present: LeAnn Rimes's first album, *Blue*. Rimes herself was only thirteen when she released her first CD. Swift was attracted to the twang of country music, and her obsession with the genre quickly grew. From iconic performers like Patsy Cline and Dolly Parton to contemporary artists, like Faith Hill, Shania Twain, and the Dixie Chicks, Swift was hooked. When Swift was eight, she saw Rimes in concert in Atlantic City. For Swift, the highlight of the evening was the moment when Rimes reached out and touched the young fan's hand. She bragged about it for an entire year to her friends.

On the Stage

After her opera-singing grandmother took Swift to see a musical adaptation of *Charlie and the Chocolate Factory*, Swift was bitten by the acting bug, too. In an interview with *Rolling Stone*, Swift recalled, "I started doing kids' musicals, because I loved seeing these kids up there singing and acting. It affected me more than I realized."

When Swift was nine, she starred in several productions at the Berks Youth Theatre Academy. The tall, confident performer landed lead roles as Kim in *Bye Bye Birdie*, Sandy in *Grease*, and Maria in *The Sound of Music*. Even on stage, Swift added a country twang to the songs she sang. Swift loved musical theater and traveled to New York City to audition for roles on Broadway. While Swift liked performing, she loved the after-performance parties even more—a karaoke machine gave her a mic, an audience, and a whole catalog of country songs to croon.

The Karaoke Circuit

At ten, Swift started performing karaoke at Henry's Restaurant during the family's annual summer vacations in Stone Harbor, New Jersey.

While Swift enjoyed performing on stage, she always preferred country songs to show tunes.

Back in Pennsylvania, her karaoke craze continued. Most weekends, Swift could be found performing onstage at festivals or in local bars, restaurants, and coffeehouses. For over a year and a half, she religiously traveled to nearby Strausstown to take part in a weekly karaoke contest held at a roadhouse owned by Pat Garrett, a local country singer. Following a win singing LeAnn Rimes's "Big Deal" at the roadhouse, Swift was given the opportunity to be the opening act for the Charlie Daniels Band when they performed at Garrett's amphitheater. She was a very early opening act; Swift performed at 10 a.m., while the Charlie Daniels Band didn't come onstage until 8 p.m.

When Swift was eleven, she watched an episode of *Behind the Music* featuring country superstar Faith Hill. Hill had moved to Nashville, Tennessee, at nineteen, where she received her big break on the country music scene. Swift decided then and there that she was going to move to Nashville to hit it big, too. Nashville, better known in the industry as Music City, is where most country performers head to launch their careers. In country, Swift found a medium that perfectly blended her love of writing and music: "I felt there were more stories told … stories that I could latch on to and be on the edge of my seat [listening to] from the beginning of the song to the end." Swift defined country music in simple terms, as: "when someone sings about their life and what they know, from an authentic place."

Music City

Nashville is widely considered to be the capital of country music. Most famous artists, from Elvis Presley to Garth Brooks, got their start there or spent some time on the Nashville music circuit. Legendary sites include the Grand Ole Opry, dubbed "Nashville's most famous stage." The Opry first rose to fame as a radio station in 1925. Over the years, it has become a rite of passage for musicians to play on the Opry stage: the honor signals that they have truly arrived on the country music scene (For Swift, that moment took place during her Opry debut in September 2006.) Other Nashville landmarks include the Country Music Hall of Fame, where visitors can learn about the city's musical past, and Lower Broadway, a strip of **honky-tonk** joints where fans can enjoy live music.

Other people, including Swift's parents, picked up on her determination. One Wyomissing neighbor described the young dreamer in an interview with the *Reading Eagle*, saying, "You could sense in Taylor that she knew what she wanted and she was going to go after it, and nothing was going to hold her back. Scott was very intent on seeing her succeed, because he knew that she had the talent."

Road Trip

After begging her parents for months to go on a trip to Nashville, Swift, Andrea, and Austin hit the road for

Music City during spring break. While her mother and brother waited in the car, eleven-year-old Swift went door to door along Music Row delivering the **demo** CD she had burned back in Reading. The demo featured Swift singing a range of well-known songs by some of Nashville's most famous female artists: the Dixie Chicks, Dolly Parton, LeAnn Rimes, and Olivia Newton-John. Marching in to the reception of each label, she handed over the CD with a simple introduction: "Hey, I'm Taylor. I'm eleven and I want a record deal. Please call me."

Not many record companies would take an eleven-year-old seriously, and no record deal came from that first trip. However, one label did call to thank Swift for her demo and to encourage the young artist to keep trying. More determined that ever, Swift knew she needed to stand out more. She decided to write her own songs and learn how to play the guitar. While she had received her first guitar as a Christmas gift when she was eight,

Taylor Swift's Demo CD Tracks

1. "There's Your Trouble" (by the Dixie Chicks)
2. "One Way Ticket (Because I Can)" (by LeAnn Rimes)
3. "Here You Come Again" (by Dolly Parton)
4. "Hopelessly Devoted to You" (by Olivia Newton-John)

An early photograph of the future princess of pop

Swift's fingers were too small to reach the different chords. In what Swift describes as a "magical twist of fate," when she was twelve, a computer repairman taught her how to play three guitar chords. From there, she wrote and performed her first song, "Lucky You." An embarrassed grown-up Swift recalls a leaked video of her home performance as "a terrifying experience" whenever it is brought up in interviews, because in the video "I sound like a chipmunk." The determined young songwriter took her music career seriously. Swift practiced guitar for about four hours every day, often until her fingers bled. She gave herself an extra challenge by learning on a twelve-stringed guitar, which is considerably more difficult to play than a more common six-stringed guitar, simply because one of her early instructors told her she wouldn't be able to do it.

"The Star-Spangled Banner"

On April 5, 2002, Swift landed her biggest gig yet—performing the national anthem at a Philadelphia 76ers game, her favorite basketball team. Dressed in a cherry-red headband and cardigan paired with a stars-and-stripes T-shirt, a nervous Swift belted out the "Star-Spangled Banner" in front of her first stadium audience. Rap superstar Jay-Z happened to be sitting courtside that day and gave Swift a high five after her performance. She knew, however, that the next day at school would be tough.

In rural Pennsylvania, country music was not especially popular, particularly among young girls. At school, Swift's deep-rooted love of country made her stand out. She was not like most girls her age who were concerned with boys and weekend sleepovers. Instead, Swift spent her weekends performing on the karaoke circuit, writing music, and making trips to Nashville. At school, Swift became an outcast, with girls leaving the lunch table when she sat down and making fun of her taste in music.

Songwriting gave Swift an escape from these difficult middle-school experiences—and plenty of material to channel into her songs. Her song "The Outside," explores

Team Taylor

Andrea and Scott were always supportive of Swift's dreams. Mother and daughter share an especially close bond. Even when Swift did not have many friends at school, she could always rely on her mom: "My mom and I have always been really close. She's always been the friend that was always there. There were times when, in middle school and junior high, I didn't have a lot of friends. But my mom was always my friend. Always."

Swift values the different traits her parents bring to both her personal and her professional life:

> I have a logical, practical, realistic mother, and a head-in-the-clouds, friendly, optimistic father. And so I'm a dreamer, and my imagination goes to places where love lasts forever and everything is covered in glitter, and that's from my dad's personality. Every time I walk off stage, he tells me how much he loved it, or how he was standing at the soundboard, crying. But my mom, she'll tell me exactly what she saw. If she saw something that could have been better, she's not going to hold it in. She's not going to sugarcoat.

Andrea and Scott often join their daughter on the road. Here, they have just touched down during the Japanese leg of the Red Tour.

this loneliness. On the jacket of her self-titled CD, which included the song, Swift gave her fans a bit of background on the lyrics:

> *This is one of the first songs I ever wrote, and it talks about the very reason I ever started to write songs. It was when I was twelve years old, and a complete outcast at school. I was a lot different than all the other kids, and I never really knew why. I was taller, and sang country music at karaoke bars and festivals on weekends while other girls went to sleepovers. Some days I woke up not knowing if anyone was going to talk to me that day.*

Bigger and Better

Swift never lost sight of her dream of becoming a country star. To perform in front of large audiences, she continued grabbing any opportunity to sing the national anthem, anytime she could. It was an effective way to get in front of a sizeable audience. Her mother was friendly with the president of the US Tennis Association, and through her connections, Swift landed a gig performing the anthem at the US Open. That day, Dan Dymtrow, the onetime business manager of pop sensation Britney Spears, happened to be in the stands. He took notice of Swift's talent and got in touch with the family. Soon, he became Swift's manager.

When Swift was thirteen, she landed a **development deal** with RCA, a smaller company owned by music powerhouse Sony Records. A development deal is not a record deal, but it does give an artist time in the studio and the opportunity to work with some of the industry's top producers and songwriters. It also allows a label time to see if a performer shows enough promise to be offered a contract for a record deal. In March 2004, Swift traveled to RCA's head office in New York City. After signing her name on the dotted line, it was official— Swift had landed her first professional gig in the music business. That year, Swift started to gain traction as an artist under the management of Dymtrow. Her song "The Outside" was included on a compilation called *Chicks with Attitude,* put out by the cosmetics company Maybelline.

With Swift's career picking up momentum, the family realized it was time for the budding songbird to spread her wings outside their small town of Reading. It was time to head to Nashville to follow in the footsteps of Swift's idols. With her whole family's support, the Swifts sold their homes in Pennsylvania and Stone Harbor, packed their bags, and headed south. Next stop: Music City, USA.

CHAPTER TWO

Gone Country

I n Tennessee, the Swifts settled in Hendersonville, a suburb of Nashville. Swift started her freshman year at nearby Hendersonville High School. After the loneliness of Pennsylvania, she found the students at her new school to be much more accepting, recalling how she didn't feel like an outcast for the first time in her life. In Nashville, the heartland of the music industry, country music was everywhere. Swift fit in quickly, and during her first week at Hendersonville High, she sang in the school's talent show. (The song was "Our Song," which would later be one of the top singles on her first album.) It was in first- period English class during freshman year that Swift met lifelong best friend Abigail Anderson, who later served as the inspiration behind Swift's hit song "Fifteen."

Swift performs in her trademark dress and cowboy boots in 2007

After school, Swift headed into downtown Nashville to the recording studio. Studio executives in Music City signed artists who, they believed, would appeal to the main demographic in country music: thirty-five-year-old women. The young songwriter knew her youth would be a factor in others not taking her work seriously. She was determined to prove them wrong—and to prove that there was a market for her songs. In an interview with the *New York Times*, Swift explained:

> *I knew every writer I wrote with was pretty much going to think, "I'm going to write a song for a fourteen-year-old today." So I would come into each meeting with five to ten ideas that were solid. I wanted them to look at me as a person they were writing with, not a little kid.*

A song idea might pop into Swift's head at any given moment, and she filled her high-school notebooks with lyrics. In between classes, she would record snippets of melodies as voice memos on her cell phone. (Swift still uses her phone for much of her songwriting; her *1989* album included three tracks to show her fans how she puts a song together using these voice memos.)

At the studio, Swift began to make connections on the Nashville music scene. Swift and producer Nathan Chapman clicked, and they began working together to lay down demo tracks. Swift landed a new gig writing songs with Sony/ATV in the spring of 2005. At thirteen, she was the youngest songwriter ever to have been hired by the publishing house. After a year of working with RCA, Swift was offered a renewal on her contract. However, the label wanted her to sing songs written by other people, and to wait a few years before putting out her first record. For Swift, that wouldn't do.

Walking away from one of the largest companies in Nashville was not something most aspiring stars would do. But for Swift, it was the right move. In an interview with the *Telegraph*, Swift explained part of her rationale for walking away:

> *I genuinely felt that I was running out of time. I'd written all these songs, and I wanted to capture these years of my life on an album while they still represented what I was going through.*

Talking about her early contracts, Swift understood the perspective of the record companies—she just didn't agree: "I can understand. They were afraid to put out a thirteen-year-old. They were afraid to put out a fourteen-year-old. Then they were afraid to put out a fifteen-year-old. Then they were nervous about putting out a sixteen-year-old. And I'm sure if I hadn't signed with Scott Borchetta [head of Big Machine Records], everybody would be afraid to put out a seventeen-year-old."

By 2005, Swift was fairly well known on the Nashville scene. She waited, somewhat impatiently, for the right deal to come along. She performed at different establishments around the city, such as the Bluebird Café. The Bluebird has been a Nashville landmark since it first opened its doors in 1982. To keep the focus on the music, the Bluebird enforces a strict no-talking policy while artists are performing. The historic café is featured in nearly every episode of ABC's TV show *Nashville*, which focuses on the country-music scene in Music City. (Swift's record label produces the music for the show.) But not all stories out of the Bluebird are fictional. In 1987, Garth Brooks was discovered playing at the café, and Faith Hill was spotted a few years later while singing backup. Soon a new artist would be discovered at the café, too. In 2005, at one of the Bluebird's acoustic **showcases** for songwriters, Swift performed some of her own material in front of an audience packed with record company executives, including Scott Borchetta. That night would prove to be life changing for the teenage songbird.

Borchetta was on the hunt for new talent. He was well established in the Nashville music scene, and had a plan in the works to leave his job as an executive at Universal to start his own **indie** label. After Swift's set, Borchetta approached her. He wanted to sign her! There was, however, a catch: his label didn't yet exist. He still needed to set up an office and secure financing. But when everything was ready to go, he promised Swift her long-awaited dream: a record deal. Two weeks later, Borchetta's phone rang: It was Swift, and she told him that she was ready to sign with him.

Swift became the first artist to sign with Borchetta's new label, Big Machine Records. Her father, Scott, recognized the fledgling business as a solid investment and became a 3 percent stakeholder. During the last four months of 2005, Swift headed into the studio to start work on her first album.

Swift and Borchetta accept the Album of the Year award for *Fearless* at the 2009 ACM Awards in Las Vegas, Nevada.

While laying down the tracks for her first album, it took a few tries to find the right partnership. Swift continuously cycled back to Nathan Chapman, the producer she had worked with in a "little shed" behind the Sony/ATV offices. The two had grown close while working on Swift's demo tracks. There was some hesitation at Big Machine about using Chapman, but Swift was persistent. While she learned a lot from working with other producers, she felt like she had better chemistry with Chapman, even though he had less experience. By the time the record was finished, Swift had proven her point. Chapman ended up producing fourteen of the fifteen tracks.

Taylor Swift

Swift's favorite song by Tim McGraw, "Can't Tell Me Nothing," inspired her own debut single, aptly titled "Tim McGraw." The song was inspired by one of Swift's freshman romances. She was dating a senior and knew they would part ways once he went off to college. The song looks back fondly on the relationship, with lines like "When you think Tim McGraw / I hope you think my favorite song / The one we danced to all night long / The moon like a spotlight on the lake." Swift cowrote the ballad, which was released on June 19, 2006, with Liz Rose, a veteran songwriter on the Nashville music scene.

In an industry where the name Tim McGraw carries a lot of sway, the single was sure to draw attention—and

Tim McGraw Meets "Tim McGraw"

At the 2007 Academy of Country Music Awards (ACMs), Swift met Tim McGraw—the artist who had inspired her breakout song—for the first time. In a special performance during the awards ceremony, Swift stepped out into the audience to where McGraw and his wife Faith Hill were seated. At the end of the song, Swift stretched out her hand and introduced herself: "Hi, I'm Taylor." A hug and lifelong friendship shortly followed.

In 2007, Swift first met country artists Tim McGraw and Faith Hill. She joined the pair later that year as an opening act on the second leg of their Soul2Soul Tour.

it did. It quickly became clear that thirty-five-year-old women were not the only fans of country music. Country Music Television (CMT) executive Brian Phillips summed up the success of the song: "From the moment 'Tim McGraw' hit the channel, [Taylor Swift] began to amass an audience that traditional Nashville didn't know or didn't believe existed, and that is young women, specifically teens."

"Tim McGraw" reached number forty on the Billboard Hot 100, altogether spending forty weeks on the chart. The song topped out in the number six slot on the Hot Country Songs Chart. In August, Swift filmed her first music video for the song, which the following year won for Breakthrough Video of the Year at the CMT Awards.

There were no guarantees that "Tim McGraw" would receive airtime. To get the attention of radio stations, Swift and her mom stuffed envelopes with promotional demo CDs. With every envelope, Swift whispered a little prayer that whoever received it would listen to it and give her a chance.

Radio Tour

Soon, Swift and Andrea hopped in the car and set out on a radio tour to promote her new song and upcoming album release. At the stations, Swift would perform her songs for rooms filled with disc jockeys (DJs). Her quirky sense of humor and girl-next-door attitude put her at ease behind the mic. Swift added an extra special touch to many of her visits by showing up with a tin of freshly baked cookies. She threw herself into the tour: "Radio tours for most artists last six weeks. Mine lasted six months. That's because I wanted it to. I wanted to meet every single one of the people that was helping me out." On air, Swift performed her songs and answered call-in questions from fans.

In the final days of her radio road trip, Swift was invited by country trio Rascal Flatts to open nine shows on their Me and My Gang tour. Within two days she was on the road again, headed for Omaha, Nebraska. She stayed with the tour until its final show in Albany, New York. With her career taking off, Swift left Hendersonville High to be homeschooled. While on the road, she completed her courses by correspondence through Aaron Academy and would graduate two years later with a 4.0 grade point average.

The First Album

On October 24, 2006, her first album, *Taylor Swift*, was released. The album sold thirty-nine thousand copies in its first week on store shelves. On the day of the album's launch, Swift appeared on *Good Morning America* with a live performance of "Picture to Burn." As more and more people heard Swift's songs, album sales began to climb; by the end of January 2007, the album had gone **gold**, meaning it had sold five hundred thousand copies. By

At the 2007 CMAs, seventeen-year-old Swift sparkled onstage while performing "Our Song."

June, less than a year after its release, *Taylor Swift* went **platinum** with over one million copies sold.

Songs from the Heart

Like "Tim McGraw," Swift's second single, "Teardrops on My Guitar," was a confession of her young love life at Hendersonville High. It was about a boy she had a crush on who already had a girlfriend. The single was released on February 19, 2007. Three more singles were released from *Taylor Swift*: "Our Song," "Picture to Burn," and "Should've Said No." All the songs performed well in

Taylor Swift: *The Track List*

1. "Tim McGraw"
2. "Picture to Burn"
3. "Teardrops on My Guitar"
4. "A Place in This World"
5. "Cold as You"
6. "The Outside"
7. "Tied Together with a Smile"
8. "Stay Beautiful"
9. "Should've Said No"
10. "Mary's Song (Oh My My My)"
11. "Our Song"
12. "I'm Only Me When I'm With You"
13. "Invisible"
14. "A Perfectly Good Heart"

the charts; "Our Song" later earned Swift recognition as the youngest person to write and sing a number-one hit on the Hot Country Songs chart. All five singles went platinum.

Swift took the country world by storm. Riding on the success of her debut album, she headed out on the road as the opening act for country's sweethearts Tim McGraw and Faith Hill and other legendary artists, including George Strait, Brad Paisley, and Kenny Chesney.

The Horizon Award

At the 2007 Country Music Awards (CMAs), Swift was presented with the Horizon Award, which is given to country music's best new artist. The prestigious award has previously been won by country heavyweights like Keith Urban, Garth Brooks, and Brad Paisley. Through tears of joy, Swift gave her acceptance speech:

> I can't even believe this is real. I want to thank God and my family for moving to Nashville so that I could do this, and I want to thank country radio. I will never forget the chance you took on me. Brad Paisley, thank you for letting me tour with you. Scott Borchetta, everybody at Big Machine Records and the fans. You have changed my life. I can't even believe this. This is definitely the highlight of my senior year!

With the industry's support and a swath of fans, no one could deny that Taylor Swift had made it.

Connecting with Fans

Swift grew up in a technologically connected world. Social media became an outlet for Swift and her fans to connect online. While working on her first album, Swift kept in touch with her growing fan base through MySpace, one of the first social networking sites to become popular during the mid-2000s. Swift spent hours each day online, reading comments and replying to fans. She also posted several clips as a video diary, chronicling her first year in the spotlight. Since then, she has used other platforms like Tumblr, Twitter, and Instagram to stay connected to her fans.

Extended Plays

Just one year after the release of *Taylor Swift*, Swift released two **extended play** (EP) albums. For the 2007 holiday season, she recorded **covers** of Christmas songs, as well as two original tunes, which were included on a holiday compilation called *The Taylor Swift Holiday Collection*. The CD was originally given an exclusive Target release, but in later years it was rereleased and made available for digital download. In July 2008, Big Machine Records partnered with Walmart for the exclusive release of a second EP called *Beautiful Eyes*. The CD was packaged with a DVD, featuring Swift's music videos, and was only available in Walmart stores. The album reached number nine on the Billboard 200.

CHAPTER THREE

Going Fearless

Following the success of her debut album, Swift soon geared up to start work on her sophomore record. She was determined to prove to her fans, followers, the industry, and herself that she was not just a one-hit wonder.

Fearless

Swift wrote or cowrote all the tracks on her second album, *Fearless*, and once again teamed up with Liz Rose to work on some new material. Rose reflected on Swift's talent for writing to *Rolling Stone* magazine, stating, "I let her say what she wants to say. People used to tell me, 'You're more like an editor with Taylor,' and it used to

Swift at work in the studio in Nashville, Tennessee.

frustrate me, because I can write lyrics, too. But those people were right. Taylor is good because she has lyrics that work for her age. I just help her grab the ones that are great."

Armed with her new songs, Swift headed back into the studio to start recording, once again with Nathan Chapman at her side. This time around, Swift was more involved on the production side; she was listed as coproducer for all thirteen of the album's tracks. Although rooted in country, many of Swift's songs had **crossover** appeal and quickly caught on with fans of the pop music genre.

Fans couldn't wait to get their hands on *Fearless*. In the five weeks leading up to the release, Swift released one single a week to give fans a taste of what was to come. *Fearless* dropped on November 11, 2008. To promote the album, Swift made her first

Swift struck a pose on the sidewalk as she arrived at the set of the *Late Show with David Letterman* to promote *Fearless*.

Fearless: The Platinum Edition

1. "Jump Then Fall"
2. "Untouchable"
3. "Forever & Always"
4. "Come In With the Rain"
5. "Superstar"
6. "The Other Side of the Door"
7. "Fearless"
8. "Fifteen"
9. "Love Story"
10. "Hey Stephen"
11. "White Horse"
12. "You Belong with Me:
13. "Breathe" (sung with Colbie Caillat)
14. "Tell Me Why"
15. "You're Not Sorry"
16. "The Way I Loved You"
17. "Forever & Always"
18. "The Best Day"
19. "Change

appearance on the *Late Show with David Letterman*. At midnight, Swift herself headed to the Hendersonville Walmart to buy her album. During the week of the album's release, the growing number of fans joining "Taylor Nation" purchased 596,000 copies of *Fearless*.

As with her first album, the songs told relatable stories about high-school friendships and teenage

Swift and then-boyfriend Joe Jonas at the 2008 MTV Video Music Awards

romances. Some tracks drew more attention from the media than others. With her growing celebrity status, Swift's love life was no longer reserved to the pages of her diary. In 2008, she was romantically linked to pop star Joe Jonas of the Jonas Brothers. People speculated that the *Fearless* song "Forever & Always" reflected on their breakup.

No matter who had inspired what song, Swift delivered an album that took the music scene by storm. *Fearless* met with favorable reviews, with *Rolling Stone's* critic giving the album four out of five stars. Reviewer Jody Rosen praised Swift's songwriting prowess, writing "[Swift's] music mixes an almost impersonal professionalism—it's so rigorously crafted it sounds like it has been scientifically engineered in a hit factory—with confessions that are squirmingly intimate and true."

The Fearless Tour

In April 2009, Swift set out on her first **headlining** tour to promote *Fearless*. Having opened for so many other artists, Swift was excited to have creative control over the theatrics of the show. The Fearless Tour included fifty-two performances, most of which sold out in minutes. For the lucky fans who were able to get tickets, they were in for quite the show.

The show opened with "You Belong with Me." Swift made her first appearance in a band uniform that was ripped off partway through the song to reveal a glittering dress beneath. Numerous costume changes, smoke machines, and huge sets brought each song to life.

During the New York City stop of the Fearless Tour, Swift energetically strutted across the stage while performing the opening number, "You Belong With Me."

During each concert, Swift would walk out into the audience, hugging fans. She recalled how that was her favorite part of each of her shows. Swift played a sparkling silver guitar, accompanied by dramatic swings of her blonde, curly hair. Always thinking of her fans, Swift had a second stage, known as a B stage in the music industry, set up at the back of the concert hall. This way, she could still connect with fans who sat in some of the worst seats in the house.

Welcome to the T-Party

Before each show, lucky fans were picked from the crowd to come backstage to meet Swift after the concert. Called the "T-Party," fans could play ping-pong, watch TV, have some snacks, and meet the pop star in a Moroccan-themed tent. The guests invited to the T-Party were usually picked out of the audience by Swift's mom.

Andrea was along for her daughter's tour, earning herself the nickname "Mama Swift." When Scott was at a show, he was known as "Daddy Swift." On tour, Scott may have been the biggest "T-Swift" fan of all. Swift described her proud dad's candid involvement: "My dad is like a kid in a candy store walking around my concerts. He walks around with guitar picks in his pocket and gives them to people. And he sells T-shirts in the T-shirt booth."

Swift is especially close with her mother, stating, "My mom and I have always been best friends." One of the tracks off Swift's first album, "The Best Day," was

Rocking Out with Taylor

In 2009, Swift made her video game debut in *Band Hero*, a spinoff of the earlier release *Guitar Hero*. In the game, players could become Swift and her band mates, jamming to tracks off *Fearless* such as "Love Story" and "You Belong with Me," as well as some earlier hits like "Picture to Burn." For the superstar, it was yet another way to connect with her fans: "Anything that encourages people to pick up an instrument and play, I'm fully behind ... This is one of the closest things out there to going to see me perform!"

written for Andrea. Swift gave a surprise performance of the song in Andrea's honor on Mother's Day during the Fearless Tour, reminiscing about her idyllic childhood, singing "I grew up in a pretty house / And I had space to run / And I had the best days with you."

At the end of the tour, Swift gave her crew members a yearbook filled with snapshots from the adventure they had all shared. She also rewarded her crew and their families with a much-deserved trip to the Bahamas. The tour was documented and later released as a movie, *Journey to Fearless*.

From Music to Movies

In 2008, Swift experienced a high-school rite of passage, senior prom—just not at Hendersonville High. With her star rapidly on the rise, Swift was featured as the surprise celebrity dream date on MTV's reality show *Once Upon A Prom*. Swift's episode was filmed down south at Hillcrest High School in Tuscaloosa, Alabama. There, senior boys sent in audition videos so Swift could choose her date. For the show, Swift and her close friend Abigail joined the Hillcrest seniors for an evening of dinner and dancing. In a generous act, Swift later donated a prom dress to a now-defunct site called DonateMyDress.org, raising $1,200 for charity.

In 2009, Swift landed her first movie role in the romantic comedy *Valentine's Day*. She was cast as the infatuated high-school sweetheart of *Twilight* star Taylor Lautner. Sparks between the two Taylors flew both on and off the set, and the pair briefly dated at the end of 2009. Swift later wrote about the relationship in "Back to December."

In January 2009, Swift made her first appearance as a musical guest on the sketch comedy show *Saturday Night Live*. Later that year, in November, she returned to New York City to make a second appearance. Swift pulled double duty this time, both hosting and performing. During the show's opening scene, she performed a comical monologue song, "Monologue Song (La La La)," which she wrote herself. Swift used her trademark sense of humor to poke fun at some of her more publicized moments, including her twenty-seven-second breakup over the phone with Joe Jonas, singer Kayne West's infamous interruption of her MTV Video Music Award

The paparazzi captured a picture of the two Taylors after a dinner date in Beverly Hills, California.

acceptance speech, and her rumored relationship with Taylor Lautner.

Swift has been a longtime fan of dramas and crime shows. (Her two cats are named after two of her favorite TV characters; Meredith, from *Grey's Anatomy*; and Olivia, from *Law and Order: SVU*.) In March 2009, Swift tried her hand at TV acting with a guest appearance on another of her favorite programs, *CSI: Las Vegas*. In the episode, called "Turn, Turn, Turn," Swift plays a young girl named Haley who ends up being murdered by her mother.

In 2012, Swift voiced the character of Audrey in the animated motion picture *The Lorax*. It was an entirely new experience for Swift—and one she loved. In 2014, she once again appeared on the big screen as Rosemary in the movie adaptation of *The Giver*. In Swift's scene, she got to show off her musical skills on the piano.

And the Winner Is ...

When awards season approached, *Fearless* was nominated for a slew of sparkling statues. While Swift had stood on the Grammy stage the year before when she performed a heartfelt duet of "Fifteen" with fellow country artist Miley Cyrus, this was the first year she was up for any awards. She was nominated in four categories, including one of the music industry's top awards: Album of the Year. In a dream-come-true moment, Swift's name was announced. In total, Swift took home two awards from the Grammys: Best Album of the Year and Best Country Album.

Other awards for *Fearless* included an Academy of Country Music (ACM) prize for Album of the Year and five wins at the American Music Awards (AMAs) for Favorite Country Album, Favorite Country Female Artist, Artist of the Year, and Favorite Country Female Artist. Swift also received recognition from *Billboard* for Top Country Album, Top Country Artist, and top performance on the Billboard 200 at their annual awards ceremony.

Stealing the Show

In September 2009, the MTV's Video Music Awards (VMAs) were held at Radio City Music Hall in New York City. Swift was nominated for Best Female Video for "You Belong with Me," a notable achievement for a self-proclaimed country artist. She was up against some of the

Kanye West stormed the stage during Swift's acceptance speech at the 2009 MTV VMAs.

industry's most successful pop stars, including Beyoncé, Kelly Clarkson, Lady Gaga, Katy Perry, and Pink.

After her landmark win was announced, an overjoyed Swift headed up to receive the fan-voted award and give her acceptance speech. Just seconds later, rapper Kanye West appeared at her side, taking the microphone away from Swift and announcing: "Yo, Taylor, I'm really happy for you, I'll let you finish, but Beyoncé has one of the best videos of all time. One of the best videos of all time!"

West handed the mic back to a shocked Swift and stalked offstage. A chorus of loud boos followed his interruption. Once backstage, Swift burst into tears. But the show had to go on; in a few minutes she was due back on stage to perform. Shaking it off, Swift rocked her performance on a reconstructed NYC subway set. Beyoncé later invited Swift back on stage to finish her acceptance speech and enjoy her moment.

The backlash against West was instantaneous. Celebrities took to Twitter defending Swift while the media criticized West. He made several public apologies for his outburst and spent time abroad while the storm blew over. While in the moment Swift was shaken, she was later able to look back at the incident with a sense of humor; she has a framed photograph of the moment, complete with a caption that reads, "Life is full of little interruptions."

In typical Swift fashion, she put the experience into song. At the 2010 VMAs, Swift chose to sing a song— "Innocent"—which was rumored to be about West. The performance opened with footage showing West's infamous grab of the mic. Lines such as "Life is a tough crowd / 32 [West's age in 2010] and still growing up now" and "Time turns new flames to embers / You'll have new Septembers" show Swift's decision to forgive and forget.

Swift and West have since become friendly; in 2015, she presented him with the Video Vanguard Award, which is given to an artist who has had a lasting impact on the MTV music scene. In her presentation speech, Swift brought the incident full circle, saying "I first met Kanye West six years ago—at this show, actually! … I have been a fan of his for as long as I can remember because Kanye defines what it means to be a creative force in music, fashion and, well, life. So I guess I have to say to all the other winners tonight: I'm really happy for you, and I'mma let you finish, but Kanye West has had one of the greatest careers of all time!"

Not-so Pitch Perfect

The 2010 Grammy Awards were a big night for Swift. At just twenty, she won the highly coveted Grammy for Album of the Year for *Fearless*. She also scooped up three more awards closer to her country roots: Best Country Song and Best Female Country Vocal Performance, both for "White Horse," and Best Country Album for *Fearless*.

That night, Swift performed a duet alongside pop-rock legend Stevie Nicks, the lead vocalist of Fleetwood Mac. The duo sang three songs: Swift's "Today Was a Fairytale," Fleetwood Mac's "Rhiannon," and Swift's "You Belong with Me." Swift's off-pitch performance came under intense scrutiny from critics. Borchetta was quick to defend his artist. Citing technical difficulties and an off night, he reminded critics of what Swift does best—connect: "When she says something, when she sings something, when she feels something, it affects more people than anybody else." Swift took the criticism in stride and began to work with a vocal coach to address some of the pitch issues. In 2010, Swift also became the new face of CoverGirl makeup, serving as the spokesperson for a new line of cosmetics called NatureLuxe. While some artists may have been content to stop there, Swift was just getting started on her climb to the top.

CHAPTER FOUR

World Domination

The young songbird still had plenty to say. Swift's third album, *Speak Now*, was released on October 25, 2010, selling over one million copies during its first week in stores. Swift wrote all of the tracks alone. This new material showed that the artist was growing up. Scott Borchetta, in an interview, recalled changing the original album name from *Enchanted* to *Speak Now:* He explained that Swift was no longer in high school and writing about fairy tales anymore, and that this album should be different. A few minutes later, Swift came up with the name that would stick.

Country music had given Swift so much that she wanted to return the favor. In May 2011, Swift

Swift displaying her lucky number thirteen in the film *Valentine's Day* (2010).

announced a four million dollar donation to the Country Music Hall of Fame and Museum in Nashville. The money was put toward a new education center that included three classrooms and interactive exhibits for budding young musicians. On October 12, 2013, Swift snipped the red ribbon, officially opening the Taylor Swift Education Center. The museum has also hosted special exhibits on Swift's career, including a special exhibit featuring memorabilia from the Speak Now World Tour.

The Speak Now World Tour started on familiar ground, in Nashville, but traveled all around the world. The massive tour included 111 shows, with stops in 82 cities. In each city, Swift performed a song by a hometown artist. More than 1.5 million fans packed

Lucky Thirteen

During the Speak Now World Tour, Swift marked her hand with her lucky number—thirteen—and scrawled song lyrics down her left arm. The number thirteen has marked some important milestones in Swift's life: she was born on December 13, landed her first recording deal at thirteen, and the introduction to her first single "Tim McGraw" lasted for thirteen seconds. Swift had said that if she were to ever get a tattoo, it would be the number thirteen, although she has no plans to get inked anytime soon.

into arenas and stadiums to see the show. Swift played six different instruments during each concert, including electric, acoustic, and twelve-stringed guitars, ukulele, piano, and a bell.

Decoding Taylor's Lyrics

Swift's love life has been a feature of her work since her debut album. Many of her songs are reminiscent of diary entries. From angst-ridden ballads about high-school sweethearts to some of her more public romantic interests, she has always refused to directly reveal much about her personal life. She has, however, buried clues, such as initials and names, into her album liners for fans to decipher.

As soon as Swift releases a new single, the media is quick to connect its subject to one of the singer's love interests. On *Speak Now*, the third track, "Back to December," was linked to Swift's whirlwind romance with her *Valentine's Day* costar Taylor Lautner.

Swift launched her new fragrance Wonderstruck at a Macy's store in New York City in October 2011.

Wonderstruck

The themes of *Speak Now* carried over into Swift's branding as well. In October 2011, Swift **endorsed** a new perfume released by Elizabeth Arden. The fragrance name, Wonderstruck, is pulled from a line of "Enchanted"—"I'm wonderstruck / blushing all the way home." Since then, Swift has released three more fragrances: Wonderstruck Enchanted (2012), Taylor (2013), and Incredible Things (2014).

"Dear John" was taken as a vengeful jab at a brief fling between Swift and singer-songwriter John Mayer. "Last Kiss" is believed by some to be a throwback to the singer's teenage romance with Joe Jonas.

Eyes on the Prize

Swift was gaining recognition from all sides of the music industry. In December 2011, she received one of the highest honors of the music industry: she was named *Billboard*'s Woman of the Year. At just twenty-one, she was the youngest person ever to receive the honor. She also locked in top awards for Top Country Artist and Top Country Album. With *Speak Now* flying up the charts, Swift also received the Billboard 200 award.

The songs on *Speak Now* also performed well at award shows. The song "Mean" earned Swift the Grammy for Best Country Solo Performance and Best Country song.

At the People's Choice Awards, she won for Favorite Country Artist, which she also secured at the AMAs, along with Favorite Country Album and Album of the Year.

Seeing Red

In 2012, the *Red* era began. In an interview with MTV, Swift discussed the significance of "red emotions" to her new set of songs, saying, "Red is the theme of the moment." She explained how "each song stands on its own musically, sonically, and emotionally too. It's kind of a patchwork quilt of all these different styles that have influenced me in one way or another."

Swift's fourth album, titled after her signature color, was released on October 22, 2012. The new record featured collaborations with Northern Irish rock band Snow Patrol and British singer-songwriter Ed Sheeran. It was also given a new pop sound by two Swedes: legendary producer Martin Shellback and songwriter Max Martin. With the new direction of the album, people were beginning to see Swift more as a pop artist than a country singer only. Swift's favorite track off the new record was the decidedly pop-sounding "I Knew You Were Trouble."

Singing with the Greats

The 1988 hit "You're So Vain" by Carly Simon publicly called out one of the singer's exes with the well-known line "You're

so vain / You probably think this song is about you." Simon
has never publicly named who inspired these lyrics. Simon
joined Swift onstage to perform the song on the Red Tour at

Red: The Deluxe Album *Track List*

1. "State of Grace"
2. "Red"
3. "Treacherous"
4. "I Knew You Were Trouble"
5. "All Too Well"
6. "22"
7. "I Almost Do"
8. "We Are Never Ever Getting Back Together"
9. "Stay Stay Stay"
10. "The Last Time" (sung with Gary ightbody, the lead vocalist for Snow Patrol)
11. "Holy Ground"
12. "Sad Beautiful Tragic"
13. "The Lucky One"
14. "Everything Has Changed" (sung with Ed Sheeran)
15. "Starlight"
16. "Begin Again"
17. "The Moment I Knew"
18. "Come Back ... Be Here"
19. "Girl at Home"
20. "Treacherous" (original demo)
21. "Red" (original demo)
22. "State of Grace" (acoustic)

Gillette Stadium in Foxboro, Massachusetts, and supposedly revealed who the song was about backstage to Swift after the show. Later, Swift expressed that she was thrilled to have met one of her musical idols.

Like Simon, Swift took vengeful songwriting to a whole new level on *Red* with her signature songwriting subject—the boys who have broken her heart, or she, theirs. It was becoming a running joke at award shows and in the tabloids that anyone who Swift dated would become her next victim. In a 2016 interview with *Maclean's* magazine, Simon defended the pop star, saying

[A]nybody who's as successful as Taylor is going to get raked over the coals for one thing or another. She could have gotten it for writing about mashed potatoes and the perfect gravy. She's so wonderful that she was born for the job. She's the perfect species for this time—in this century. She's the ideal girl. Which is why they want to rake her over the coals.

Having her life splashed across the headlines has led Swift to take her privacy seriously. By opening her life up to the world, Swift has given up any real sense of normalcy. In an interview with *Rolling Stone,* she described her reality: "There's someone whose entire job it is to figure out things that I don't want the world to see. They look at your career, they look at what you prioritize, and they try to figure out what would be the most revealing or hurtful." As the years have passed, Swift has developed a thicker skin so as to not take the tabloid's headlines to heart.

The Guessing Game

With the release of *Red*, fans and critics alike raced to figure out who each song was about. Swift had once dated One Direction band member Harry Styles. *Red*'s lead single, "I Knew You Were Trouble," is often attributed to their breakup. Other songs were linked to actor Jake Gyllenhaal and socialite Conor Kennedy. "Starlight" was inspired by a romantic photograph of Conor's grandparents, Ethel Kennedy and her husband, former New York State Senator Robert F. Kennedy, dancing together.

Branded Red

To promote the album, Swift made sure to highlight the color red. In most media appearances, she donned red lipstick and accessories. In 2013, Swift landed an endorsement as the new face of Keds women's footwear. The company kicked off a new campaign alongside the *Red* album launch, branded with the gutsy slogan "Here's to the brave girls." The endorsement deal also included the launch of an exclusive line of red sneakers.

That year, Swift also partnered with Diet Coke, her favorite brand of soda. She became the brand ambassador for the popular beverage and released a limited edition slim can featuring her signature and one of her favorite quotes—"If you're lucky enough to be different, don't ever change"—in cursive writing. In more recent years, some medical associations have criticized Swift for promoting Diet Coke, a product that contains aspartame, an artificial sweetener linked to some illnesses.

The Red Tour

The Red Tour kicked off in Omaha, Nebraska, in March, 2013. The starlet was growing up; she made her show entrance to singer Lenny Kravitz's remake of the song

During the Nashville leg of her Red Tour, Swift performed "All Too Well," the first song she penned for the album

"American Woman." (During the Speak Now Tour, she had used Tom's Petty's "American Girl.") On the Red Tour, the T-Party was reinvented as Club Red. Once again, Swift's fans were guaranteed their money's worth—and much more.

Iconic performances included a powerful piano piece—on a red piano, of course—during "All Too Well." Ed Sheeran made appearances at every show and even

A New Perspective

Aside from sharing her own stories, in 2012, Swift was given the chance to write from the perspective of one of her favorite literary characters: Katniss Everdeen of the best-selling *The Hunger Games* trilogy by Suzanne Collins. The movie studio was gearing up for the release of the first installment of the films based on the books. Swift, a fan of the series, was asked to write two songs specifically for the upcoming release. The ballad "Safe and Sound" was a collaboration between Swift and the country music duo The Civil Wars. "Eyes Open" was penned by Swift alone. Both songs were included on the movie soundtrack *Songs from District 12 and Beyond.* Swift took home a Grammy for "Safe and Sound" and also received a Golden Globe nomination for Best Original Song.

commemorated the experience by adding a "Red" tattoo to his arm. The Red Tour truly was a global venture, with stops in major cities across North America, Australia, Europe, and Asia. The fifteen-month tour grossed over $150 million as the top tour of the year.

Recognizing Red

At the 2013 AMAs, Swift was the fan favorite, taking the top slot as the favorite country artist. She also locked in the top prize of Artist of the Year. At the Billboard Awards, Swift's arms were full with eight awards. In one of her many acceptance speeches, Swift gave a shout-out to her fans: "Thank you for making my music the soundtrack to your crazy emotions. You are the longest and best relationship I've had." That night, she also premiered a single from *Red*, "22." The catchy song celebrates what had become an extremely successful year for Swift.

Lifetime Achievement

At the 2013 CMAs, Swift was nominated for several awards, including Entertainer of the Year and Female Vocalist of the Year. *Red* was nominated for Album of the Year, and Swift also shared nominations in three categories with Tim McGraw and Keith Urban for the trio's collaboration on "Highway Don't Care." (The threesome won for Musical Event for the Year and Music Video of the Year.)

The evening would also mark another milestone in the young artist's career: Swift was honored with the coveted Pinnacle Award. This is a lifetime achievement award that is bestowed upon an artist who has gained national and international recognition within the country music genre. She had brought new life to the country music scene and new energy to the genre. The only other person to receive the award in the history of the CMAs was Garth Brooks, in 2005. Brooks was forty-three when he received the honor; Swift was just twenty-three. She had certainly come a long way in just a few short years.

Leading up the presentation, many of the biggest names in country shared their memories of working with Swift, and their admiration for the young star. Tim McGraw summed up the feelings of the entire country community: "We have all seen her grow up into a beautiful woman and a truly global superstar." After receiving accolades from her fellow musicians, a video showed celebrities like Reese Witherspoon, Julia Roberts, Ellen DeGeneres, Justin Timberlake, and Mick Jagger congratulating Swift on her accomplishments.

Several months later, at the 2014 Grammys, *Red* was up for Album of the Year. When Alicia Keys began to read the winners, Swift thought she had won for a split second when she heard the start of an "R"— however, the award went to Daft Punk for *Random Access Memory*. Swift made a quick recovery and gave Daft Punk a standing ovation.

Swift's next album was already in the works. After losing out on Album of the Year, she took a look back at her last few albums. While the singles off *Speak Now* and *Red* had been tremendously successful, artistically Swift considered the albums to be a bit like patchwork quilts, a jumble of songs lacking a unifying and identifiable sound. Swift decided it was time to refocus on creating an album with a cohesive sound. With pop melodies running through her head and a new focus, it was time to push herself forward once again.

CHAPTER FIVE

The Rebirth of T-Swift

I t was time to shake things up—or more so, *off*—
again. In April 2014, Swift packed up and moved
from Nashville to the Big Apple. She purchased
the penthouse of a swanky building in the Tribeca
neighborhood. She also bought the apartment across
the hall to house her security team. Her new neighbors
included actor Orlando Bloom and producer
Steven Soderbergh.

"Shake It Off"

Swift was also moving in a new direction as an artist.
For the past few years, her songs had begun to sound
less country and more mainstream pop. As usual, Swift
pushed herself forward to give her fans a whole new

Swift performing during her 1989 World Tour in Tokyo.

sound. In August 2014, Big Machine Records released the first single off Swift's highly anticipated fifth studio album, *1989*. Swift's first live performance of "Shake It Off" aired at the 2014 VMAs. *Rolling Stone* reviewed the performance, declaring that it "[shredded] any threads to country music with a stunning, OCD [obsessive compulsive disorder] performance that recalls decades of pop video."

The song was largely a response to nearly a decade spent living under the microscopic eye of the media. As Swift explained to *Rolling Stone:*

I've had every part of my life dissected—my choices, my actions, my words, my body, my style, my music. When you live your life under that kind of scrutiny, you can either let it break you, or you can get really good at dodging punches. And when one lands, you know how to deal with it. And I guess the way that I deal with it is to shake it off.

The new album, *1989*, was unlike anything Swift had ever put out before. The record marked her official, wholehearted leap from country to pop. The album's thirteen tracks drew on inspiration from iconic eighties artists like Madonna and Phil Collins. This new direction met with some early resistance from the singer's label. Even the album name came under review. But as usual, Swift stuck to her guns. She knew it was the right time to make a move. "I know how to write a song," Swift said.

Excited Swifties filled the stadium at the Detroit stop for the 1989 Tour.

"I'm not confident about a lot of other aspects of my life, but I know how to write a song." When Swift sent *1989* to Borchetta, he called it said he felt it was one of the best albums she had ever done. However, there was a catch—

he still wanted three country songs to be included. But Swift stood firm. As she told *Rolling Stone*, "At a certain point, if you chase two rabbits, you lose them both." Swift had conquered the country scene; it was time to see if she could make the full leap to pop.

Some people viewed the full-fledged move from country to pop as a risky move. But for Swift and her generation of younger fans, music was no longer defined along the lines of one genre or another:

> *You're just now starting to see the generation of kids who grew up able to make their own playlist. These are the artists that are now making music and making up the landscape of mainstream music. So you have genres blending into each other as the norm … You have folk music that sounds like country used to sound like, you have pop music that sounds like blends of blues, [and] you have country music that sounds like rock.*

The country music community was sad to see Swift go. At the 2015 CMAs, which celebrated the show's fiftieth anniversary, Swift was honored with a Milestone Award. Andrea Swift presented her daughter with the award. In her acceptance speech, Swift bid a fond farewell to Nashville—for now.

The Secret Sessions

Swift wanted her fans to be the first people to hear her new music. So, ahead of the album's release, she

Fans of all ages love getting the chance to meet Swift backstage after her concerts.

organized five "secret sessions"—listening parties where her most diehard fans were treated to a sneak preview of all the new songs on *1989*. The sessions took place in Swift's houses in London, New York, Nashville, Los Angeles, and Rhode Island. For each session, eighty-nine fans, usually handpicked by Swift over social media, were sworn to secrecy. They were each promised a once-in-a-lifetime experience.

At the session in Los Angeles, Swift surprised the crowd of "Swifties" packed into her living room. She explained to them that she had handpicked each one of them and wanted to play her new album for them before anyone else listened to it. Fans were also treated to homemade cookies, baked by Swift herself. She recorded footage from the sessions and posted it to social media.

1989

On October 27, 2014, the long-anticipated wait was over: *1989* was released. Prior to its release, Billboard projected sales of about eight hundred thousand. Yet again, Swift's fans rose to the occasion, and *1989* exploded onto the music scene, selling 1.287 million copies during the week of its release. The record-breaking sales marked Swift's third album to sell more than one million copies during its first week on store shelves. People couldn't get enough of the album; it spent an entire year in the Billboard Top Ten. By July 2015, the album had gone platinum five times, making it the fastest selling record to be released in over ten years.

Taylor 2.0

Alongside the launch of *1989*, American Express, the credit card company, partnered with the princess of pop to release a new app piggybacking on the runaway success of the album's second single, "Blank Space." The free, interactive app, called "American Express Unstaged: Taylor Swift Experience," takes Swifties into the song's music video, which takes place in a real-life castle on Long Island. Users can follow the action between Swift and her love interest as they quarrel or explore the sprawling estate on their own. The app won a Primetime Emmy in 2015 for its innovative interactive experience. Another app, called TayText, gives tongue-tied users

1989: *The Track List*

1. "Welcome to New York"
2. "Blank Space"
3. "Style"
4. "Out of the Woods"
5. "All You Had to Do Was Stay"
6. "Shake It Off"
7. "I Wish You Would"
8. "Bad Blood"
9. "Wildest Dreams"
10. "How You Get the Girl"
11. "This Love"
12. "I Know Places"
13. "Clean"

access to over three hundred of Swift's most poignant lines from a catalog of sixty songs.

Behind the Music

Swift had grown tired of her personal life constantly being splashed across the tabloids and of her portrayal as a serial dater. So, as usual, she expressed her feelings through her lyrics. One of the biggest hits on *1989*, "Blank Space," is a satire about the boy-hungry girl the media has long portrayed Swift to be.

In September 2015, Swift gave a stripped-down acoustic performance of three songs off *1989* to celebrate

Swift's videos are known for their drama and theatrics. The AMEX app takes users into the story depicted in "Blank Space" where the singer plays a crazed serial dater.

the record-breaking attendance of the exhibit. Before performing "Blank Space," she explained how the song was a response to the tabloid coverage she experienced following her *Red* album:

> My first reaction was like, "This is a bummer. This isn't fun for me." But then my second reaction ended up being like, "Hey, that's a really interesting character they're writing about. She jet sets around the world collecting men ... then she traps them and locks them in her mansion, and then she's crying in her marble bathtub surrounded by pearls." So I was like, "I can use this."

The Taylor Swift Experience

You know you've hit it big when you have your own Grammy Museum exhibit. On December 13, 2014, the Grammy Museum in Los Angeles, California opened one called the Taylor Swift Experience. The exhibit chronicled Swift's path to superstardom and featured costumes from past tours, handwritten song lyrics, home videos, and other memorabilia. Visitors could even record their own covers of "We Are Never Getting Back Together." The exhibit drew crowds to the museum and, in the first quarter of 2015, attendance was up 35 percent. Based on its popularity, the Taylor Swift Experience, initially scheduled to close in May, was extended until October 2015.

1989: The Cover Album

Fans were not the only people who couldn't get the catchy tracks of *1989* out of their heads. In December 2014, while traveling on tour, singer Ryan Adams became fixated on the lyrics to Swift's songs. Her purchased a four-track cassette player and started putting his own unique twist on them. Adams's remix took *1989* in a more laidback, folksy direction, swapping out electric pop sounds for the toned-down notes of the acoustic guitar and harmonica. When he ran out of space on the recorder, Adams took his new idea into the studio, where he continued recording with backup musicians. Adams has been a longtime fan of Swift since the release of her single "White Horse." The two artists had also previously worked together on one of Swift's unreleased songs during the recording of *Red*. Adams explained his tribute to *Rolling Stone*, saying, "It's not a reimagining or a reconstruction at all. It's a parallel universe. That's how I think of it. We're creating an alternate universe, like in Marvel Comics."

After news of Adams's cover of *1989* reached Swift, it quickly met with her approval. Throughout the project, Adams was in touch with Swift, and, when recording sessions wrapped up, he sent the completed album to her before anyone else.

During the days leading up to the new album's release in September 2015, Swift tweeted: "Ryan's music helped shape my songwriting. This is surreal and dreamlike." The star of the TV show *Girls*, actress Lena Dunham, also took to Twitter, posting support on her feed for the reimagined *1989*: "Holy heck y'all. Just heard [the] *1989* cover album and it's a masterwork."]

During the week of October 10, the twin albums both reached the top ten of the Billboard 200 chart, with Swift's album moving into the eighth spot during its forty-eighth week on the chart and Adams's cover landing in seventh during its first.

On the Road, Again

On November 3, 2014, the 1989 World Tour was announced. This concert would be different than any of Swift's previous shows. In a digitally-connected world where videos leak onto the Internet, Swift wanted to give her fans an unmatchable experience at each performance. How? By having surprise celebrity guests join her onstage each night. As Swift explained:

> In this generation, I know as I'm walking on stage that a huge percentage of the crowd have already YouTubed the entire show and watched the whole thing online. They know the set list, they know the costumes, they've looked it up. That presented me with an interesting issue. I love the element of surprise ... so going into this tour, having people pop on stage that you didn't expect to see—not only musicians, but actors and athletes and models and people in every type of field.

The star-studded lineup was impressive. Swift's close pals, actress Selena Gomez and singer Lorde both made appearances. Other guests included fellow singers Alanis Morisette, Beck, Ellie Goulding, Justin Timberlake, Keith Urban, and Nelly, talk show host Ellen DeGeneres, and actresses Julia Roberts and Lisa Kudrow—to name a few. For musical guests, Swift's band members were kept on their toes; they had about thirty-five minutes to learn new material for each night's performance.

Girls Just Want to Have Fun

In an interview with radio station Beats 1, Swift reflected on the *1989* era as a whole: "I feel like this tour and this album and this phase of my life have been about inclusivity. Doing it on my own, but doing it with friends." Swift moved her love life to the back burner, instead focusing on her music and friends. She amassed a huge social circle, made up of several celebrities. She has been longtime friends with fellow performers Selena Gomez and Lorde, and in recent years, she has gained even more high-profile friends. Some friendships were spurred from chance meetings. While performing at the Victoria's Secret fashion show, Swift became close with supermodel Karlie Kloss. Others were forged over social media. Swift had been a longtime fan of writer and actress Lena Dunham. The two connected over Twitter, becoming fast friends.

Close friends Lorde, Selena Gomez, and Swift often sit together at award shows. Here, they posed for the camera at the 2014 AMAs

"Bad Blood"

Swift's *1989* collaborations with fellow stars were not just limited to her tour, however. One of the most popular tracks off *1989*, "Bad Blood" was a compilation between Swift and rapper Kendrick Lamar. The music video for "Bad Blood" took the song to a whole new level. The video features an all-star cast of characters, played by some of Swift's closest gal pals. The video premiered at the 2014 Billboard Music Awards. People have speculated that the song is about Katy Perry, although Swift, as usual, refuses to directly name who inspires her songs.

When asked what her "pinch-me moment" on the 1989 Tour was, singing with Mick Jagger stood out for Swift. Scott Swift, who always seems to have his finger on the pulse of happenings in Nashville, told his daughter the day before her show that the Rolling Stones frontman was in town. An excited Swift sent Jagger a text message, asking if he would make an appearance onstage. He coyly asked her what he should wear. The next night, fans were treated to a surprise duet of "(I Can't Get No) Satisfaction."

The 1989 Tour was the top-grossing tour of any artist in 2015, bringing in over $250 million. Every show on the tour sold out within minutes. For Swift, it was an unforgettable experience, and one that will be difficult to top.

Awards Mania

With the runaway success of 1989, 2015 proved to be a good year. The new album met with favorable reviews across the board. *Billboard and Rolling Stone* both included *1989* in their top picks for 2014. At the 2015 MVAs, "Bad Blood" won Best Video and Best Collaboration, and "Blank Space" took the top spot for Favorite Video and Favorite Pop Video. At the 2016 People's Choice Awards, Swift won awards for favorite female and favorite pop artist.

At the Billboard Music Awards, Swift led the pack with eight wins. She was named top artist and top female artist. Her recordbreaking album sales spoke for themselves, securing the top spot on the Billboard 200 and Hot 100 charts. She also led the pack as the top-selling digital artist and the top Billboard 200 artist. "Shake It Off" landed the win for the top streaming video. Swift also received the fan-voted Billboard achievement award for chart performance.

At the AMAs, "Blank Space" won for Song of the Year. *1989* wrapped up two wins for favorite pop/rock album, and Swift was named the top adult contemporary artist.

At the 2016 Grammy Awards, Swift locked in Album of the Year with 1989, becoming the first female artist to ever achieve this milestone twice, having won for Fearless back in 2010. The album also earned recognition for the Best Pop Vocal Album, and Swift shared the title of Best Music Video with Kendrick Lamar for "Bad Blood."

Haters Gonna Hate

In October 2015, Jessie Braham, an R&B singer whose stage name is Jesse Graham, contacted Swift's record label, Sony, claiming a line from one of his songs had been used in the runaway hit "Shake It Off." His song, "Haters Gone Hate," released in 2013, included the line "Haters gone hate / Players gone play." Braham requested a selfie with the star and to have his name added as a cowriter to "Shake It Off." But when the complaint was dismissed by Sony, he decided to ask for more; Braham filed a lawsuit against Swift and Sony to the tune of a substantial $42 million.

The lawsuit was, however, short-lived; in November, a judge in California ruled that Braham's case did not have enough evidence to support his claim that she'd stolen the line. In her written dismissal, Judge Gail Standish cleverly borrowed some of Swift's best-known lyrics from "We Are Never Ever Getting Back Together," "Bad Blood," and "Blank Space." She wrote: At present, the Court is not saying that Braham can never, ever, ever get his case back in court. But, for now, we have got problems, and the Court is not sure Braham can solve them. As currently drafted, the Complaint has a blank space—one that requires Braham to do more than write his name. And, upon consideration of the Court's explanation ... Braham may discover that mere pleading Band-Aids will not fix the bullet holes in his case. At least for the moment, Defendants have shaken off this lawsuit.

CHAPTER SIX

A Generous Heart and a Level Head

Aside from her runaway success as a pop superstar, Swift has also been recognized for her generous spirit and business savvy. From her early days singing country tunes about break-ups to today, Swift has prided herself on being a role model to millions of young people, particularly girls. She has always been conscious of the clothes she wears and the messages she sends through her actions and music. Swift has also used her celebrity status to bring awareness to dozens of causes and to give back to the fans she is thankful for.

Fame for Good

In 2007, Swift teamed up with the governor of Tennessee to raise awareness about the dangers of social media in

Swift poses with one of her fans.

After flooding devastated the Nashville area in 2010, country music stars joined together to give a benefit concert to raise money for the recovery efforts.

the Delete Online Predators campaign. Aimed at 150,000 middle-school-aged students, the campaign focused on education. Swift stopped in at Merrol Hyde Magnet School to talk to the students and encourage each of them to sign the NetSmartz Internet Safety Pledge.

As far back as 2008, Swift began using her newfound fame—and her growing wealth—to help others. During the summer of 2008, Swift donated the profits from merchandise sold during the CMA Music Festival to the Nashville Red Cross. In August, during a concert in Cedar Springs, Iowa, she announced a $100,000 donation to the local Red Cross to provide assistance to the towns that had been devastated by floods a few months earlier. At her eighteenth birthday party, she was given a bright-pink Chevy pickup from Big Machine, which she later donated to a camp for sick children.

The year 2008 also marked a historic presidential race between Barack Obama and John McCain. The morning of her eighteenth birthday, the first thing Swift did was register to vote. During the lead-up to Election Day, she joined forces with country legends Reba McEntire and Martina McBride to empower women to vote. The Every Woman Counts campaign set out to encourage women to take a more active role in politics, from voting to running as candidates themselves. Swift appeared in a public service announcement sharing her enthusiasm as a first-time voter.

In 2010, disaster struck close to home. Massive flooding devastated the state of Tennessee, including the Nashville area. Swift described the experience during a call-in to a telethon raising money for flood relief:

> *It was the craziest thing that I've ever seen. I was at my house in Hendersonville, we were staring out the window, thinking it didn't seem like rain. It just seemed like something in a movie. It was really emotional for me because those are the streets I learned to drive on. People's houses are just ruined. It was so heartbreaking to see that in my town, the place that I call home, and the place that I feel most safe. I just send my love to my friends and neighbors who got hit harder than I did.*

Swift made a generous donation of $500,000 to the telethon. The following year, she sang at a benefit concert to raise money for tornado relief and also donated

$250,000 toward rebuilding parts of southern Alabama that were hit by tornadoes.

Random Acts of Kindness

Swift has become well known for simple but powerful acts of kindness toward her fans. In 2015, she sent a check for $1,989 to college student Rebekah Bortnicker to put toward paying off her student loans. To give back to her loyal army of Swifties, Swift started celebrating "Swiftmas" in 2014. Swift checked in on some of her most loyal fans, researching them through social media. In what has been dubbed "Taylurking," the pop star sifts through her hardcore fans feeds on platforms such as Instagram, Tumblr, and Twitter. She then writes

In 2012, Swift paired up with ambassadors from Free the Children to switch on the Christmas lights at Westfield shopping center in London, England.

personalized cards and even hand-delivers some gifts to them for Christmas and Hanukkah.

Swift is also known for making surprise visits. In November 2014, she visited a mother and her two-year-old son in New Haven, Connecticut with some early Christmas gifts, including a miniature Mercedes for one of her youngest fans. She also often visits sick children in the hospital, bringing along her guitar for one-on-one concerts.

Standing Up for Cancer

While Swift's stories resonate with millions, she is also touched by her fans' personal experiences. Swift is always online, following the lives of her fans on social media and reading blogs. It is one way she stays connected in a life that has become far from normal. One story that had a profound effect on the songwriter was that of Ronan Thompson. Every night, Swift would read entries in a blog written by Maya Thompson, Ronan's mother. On her blog, Rockstar Ronan, Thompson chronicled the story of her four-year-old son's battle with neuroblastoma, a rare form of cancer. Swift was moved by Ronan's story. She used stories from his mother's blog to write the charity single "Ronan." Swift credits his mother as a cowriter. She first performed the song during a 2012 *Stand Up to Cancer* telethon. All of the singer's proceeds from the song go toward cancer research, including the Ronan Thompson Foundation, which was founded in Ronan's memory.

Swift gives a heartfelt performance of "Ronan." She has only publicly performed the song twice, once at the Stand Up to Cancer telethon and later in 2015 after sharing the news of her mother's cancer diagnosis.

In April 2015, "Ronan" struck a new chord with Swift as it hit close to home. On her Tumblr feed, Swift shared with her fans that her mother had been diagnosed with cancer. She kept the details private but used the post to increase awareness of health screening:

She wanted you to know because your parents may be too busy juggling everything they've got going on to go to the doctor, and maybe you reminding them to go get checked for cancer could possibly lead to an early diagnosis and an easier battle... Or peace of mind in knowing that they're healthy and there's nothing to worry about. She wanted you to know why she may not be at as many shows this tour. She's got an important battle to fight.

In August 2015, during the 1989 Tour stop in Glendale, Arizona, a visibly emotional Swift performed the song. It was a special show; Maya Thompson was in the audience.

No Bullies Allowed

Swift is always on the side of her loyal followers and ready to offer advice on anything from what to wear to prom to how to deal with bullying. As a victim of middle-school bullying herself, Swift feels a connection with many of her Swifties. She often posts encouraging messages and videos, telling her fans to be proud of who they are. In response to a fan named Caillou who was getting bullied about his name, Swift wrote back the empowering message:

> You will always be criticized and teased and bullied for things that make you different, but usually those things will be what set you apart. The things that set you apart from the pack, the things that you once thought were your weaknesses will someday become your strengths. So if they say you're weird or annoying or strange or too this or not enough that, maybe it's because you threaten them. Maybe you threaten them because you're not the norm. And if you're not the norm, give yourself a standing ovation.

A World of Possibility

In 2012, Swift worked with children's book publisher Scholastic to put books in the hands of children. Swift donated six thousand books to the library in her hometown of Reading and another fourteen thousand to libraries across Nashville. A love of words and reading opened a whole new world to Swift, fueling her childhood dreams to become a singer-songwriter. She wanted to share that passion with others. Swift revealed a few of her favorite reads to Scholastic, including the Harry Potter series, *Stargirl*, and *The Fault in Our Stars*. All of these books feature strong female characters, much like Swift herself. In November 2015, Swift teamed up with Scholastic again to donate twenty-five thousand books to schools across the five boroughs of her new hometown, New York City. The year before, Swift recorded a podcast about her love of reading that has been heard by over 4.5 million students.

A number of organizations have recognized Swift's generous spirit. In 2012, the first lady of pop met the First Lady of the United States when Michelle Obama presented Swift with the Big Help Award at the Nickelodeon Kids' Choice Awards. Later that year, Kerry and Rory Kennedy gave Swift the prestigious Ripple of Hope award. This award recognizes an individual who forges a path for social change.

A Celeb Gone Good

At the end of 2015, Swift topped DoSomething.org's "Celebs Gone Good List" for the fourth year in a row. Between touring and promoting *1989*, Swift made some extra-special donations. She gave fifty thousand dollars to a young fan named Naomi Oakes who missed a concert while battling leukemia. Swift made the donation at GoFundMe.com, an online fundraising platform. The site maxes out donations at fifteen thousand dollars, so Swift had to make four separate transactions. The website later changed its maximum donation option to fifty thousand dollars, based on the singer's generosity. The proceeds from Swift's video for "Wildest Dreams" were also all donated to the African Parks Foundation of America, an organization that heads up conservation efforts in five of Africa's national parks. Swift also gave fifty thousand dollars to a backup dancer's infant nephew for cancer treatment, and to arts programs in New York City. After hearing a recording of the Seattle Symphony Orchestra's "Become Ocean," which reminded the songbird of childhood visits to the symphony with her grandmother, Swift also donated fifty thousand dollars to the orchestra.

The Business Side of Things

Swift has risen to the top as the favorite artist of a new generation of music lovers. Since day one, when she first signed with Big Machine Records, she has taken an active role in her music—both artistically and on the business side of things. With her parent's background in finance and management, they taught Swift how to manage her business well.

Over the past ten years, the entire music industry has undergone rapid changes in how users consume music. Fans used to have to wait for a CD to be released, then go to a brick-and-mortar store to purchase it. Today, with the simple click of a button or the swipe of a finger, music is instantly available for download onto a person's laptop, smartphone, or other device. Within this new music era, music **piracy** has exploded. People can now use illegal services, which do not compensate artists for their work, to download their favorite songs. This in turn has led to the decline in sales of physical albums. (Swift's albums have largely been the exception to this rule.)

In July 2014, Swift wrote an **op-ed** that ran in the prestigious *Wall Street Journal*. For Swift, there is an important value that needs to be placed on music. She wrote,

> *Music is art, and art is important and rare. Important, rare things are valuable. Valuable things should be paid for. It's my opinion that music should not be free, and my prediction is that individual artists and their labels will someday decide what an album's price point is. I hope they don't underestimate themselves or undervalue their art.*

The value Swift places on her music has led to some publicized face-offs with some of the most popular streaming services on the market today. But as the reigning queen of pop, Swift has a lot of pull in the music business. Just days after *1989* launched, she went head-to-head with start-up streaming service Spotify. Companies like Spotify allow listeners to stream music in a number of ways. Users can pay for a premium service, usually billed at $9.99 per month, which gives them access to songs or playlists. Or they can listen to the same music for free after listening to advertisements.

Leading up to the album's launch, the artist had been in talks with Spotify to discuss some conditions regarding

Staggering Sales

Swift's staggering sales speak for themselves; over twenty-two of her songs have been downloaded more than one million times. By November 2014, according to Nielsen SoundScan, Swift's top-ten best-selling digital singles included:

"Love Story": 5.8 million
"I Knew You Were Trouble.": 5 million
"You Belong With Me": 4.5 million
"We Are Never Ever Getting Back Together":
    3.9 million
"Our Song": 3.2 million
"Teardrops on My Guitar": 2.9 million
"Shake It Off": 2.7 million
"Mean": 2.3 million
"Mine": 2.2 million
"22": 2 million

how the service would offer its users access to Swift's newest record. Swift wanted US-based users to only be able to access the album through the premium service, while fans outside of the country could have access to the album through the free service. When Spotify would not change their policies, Swift pulled all her music off the platform.

Powering Up

By the end of 2014, Swift was ranked as one of the most powerful celebrities in the world. *Forbes* magazine ranked her the eighth most powerful celebrity, and sixty-fourth on their list of the world's top players. She finished off an incredible year by celebrating her twenty-fifth birthday with another nod from Billboard: she was named the 2014 Woman of the Year. It was her second time receiving the notable award. In her acceptance speech, she reflected on her perspective as an artist in the ever-evolving music industry:

> I'm very well aware the music industry is changing, and it will continue to change. I'm open to that change and progress. I'm not open to the financial model that is currently in place. I really believe that we in the music industry can work together to bond technology with integrity. And I think we can teach a younger generation about an investment in music, not just the ephemeral consumption of it. I think that there has to be a way for streaming or any future way we access music to fairly compensate the writers.

In 2015, she took on tech giant Apple after the company launched a new streaming service, Apple Music. In the new program, users paid a monthly fee for unlimited access to thousands of songs by hundreds of artists. In contrast, on iTunes, which launched in 2003, users make a one-time purchase of a song that is downloaded to a device.

With the launch, Apple Music promoted a three-month free trial for people to test out the service before becoming paying subscribers. However, there was a catch for artists; they would not receive royalties for music that was accessed during the trial.

While she was touring in Amsterdam, Swift received a text message from a friend with the news about Apple Music's free trial. In the early morning hours, Swift wrote an open letter to Apple, addressing their decision. She posted the letter on her Tumblr page:

> *This is not about me ... This is about the new artist or band that has just released their first single and will not be paid for its success. This is about the young songwriter who just got his or her first cut and thought that the royalties from that would get them out of debt. This is about the producer who works tirelessly to innovate and create, just like the innovators and creators at Apple are pioneering in their field ... but will not get paid for a quarter of a year's worth of plays on his or her songs.*

Seventeen hours later, Apple Music announced via Twitter that it would in fact be compensating artists during the three-month trial. The media heralded Swift as a hero. The publicity led to a new relationship between Swift and the tech company. Just a few months later, Swift granted Apple the exclusive release of the 1989 World Tour documentary, which launched on Apple Music on December 20, 2015.

On to the Next ...

When you've conquered the world as the reigning princess of pop, where do you head next? After the successful 1989 Tour, Swift plans to take a well-deserved

Style Icon

From her early days in Nashville sporting sundresses and cowboy boots, Swift has become a fashion icon. During her late teens, she dressed in a more whimsical fashion. As she has grown up, Swift has moved more toward vintage styles, inspired by fashions from the 1950s and 1960s. She sums up her personal style as "feminine, experimental, and classic."

In January 2016, Swift launched her own fashion line during Hong Kong Fashion Week. She worked with Nashville-based designer Heritage66 to put together a collection that reflected her own personal style, complete with crop tops, dresses, and other pieces sprinkled with the pop star's name. The line is currently only available in China.

break in 2016. The sheer success of *1989* is going to be difficult to top; Swift told the *Telegraph* that she was concerned that she wouldn't be able to put out a better album. Someday, Swift plans to write her autobiography, putting to paper the story of her climb to the top. In her personal life, Swift has been dating Scottish DJ and producer Calvin Harris, known for his hit songs "Summer" and "Feel So Close," since March 2015.

In an article commemorating the ten-year anniversary of Big Machine Records, Borchetta reflected on Swift: "When I met her, I was just smitten. She was a fascinating person, even at fourteen years old. She had such an amazing desire for people to like her and get to know her, and she has found a way to engage anybody whom she wants to, whether it's the immediate fan or the biggest stars in the world."

As for the future, Swift aspires to have a career like two iconic women: Oprah Winfrey and Angelina Jolie. Both celebrities have spent years using their fame and wealth to help others. According to Swift:

> *If you look at Oprah, she's made so many people happy over the years. She's made so much money, but she's given so much of it away. Same thing with Angelina Jolie. She's been so productive, but she's used that position to better other people's lives, and I think that's where I'd want to be. I want to leave a trail of people behind me who had gotten better opportunities or felt better about themselves because of me or smiled because of me.*

As she has grown as both a person and an artist, Swift has kept her fans front and center. No matter where she goes from here, her fans are guaranteed songs that speak to the common experiences of people everywhere. Swift's role as a leading woman is to encourage others to discover the value in themselves. She says, "My hope for the future, not just in the music industry, but in every young girl I meet … is that they all realize their worth and ask for it."

Taylor Swift

Timeline

2005

Swift is signed to Big Machine Records by Scott Borchetta.

2001

During spring break, Swift and her mom travel to Nashville for the first time to deliver demo CDs on Music Row.

2007

Swift is presented with the Horizon Award at the CMAs.

Taylor Alison Swift is born in Reading, Pennsylvania, on December 13.

1989

Swift's first single, "Tim McGraw," is released on June 19, followed by her debut album *Taylor Swift* on October 24.

2006

Swift signs a development deal with RCA and becomes the youngest songwriter ever hired by Sony/ATV. The family moves to Nashville, Tennessee.

2004

Swift's second album, *Fearless*, is released on November 11.

2008

2012

Red is released on October 22 and goes platinum within a week.

2016

In February, 1989 earns Swift second Album of the Year win at the Grammy Awards.

2009

Fearless wins Album of the Year at the MTV VMAs, and Kanye West famously interrupts Swift's acceptance speech.

2014

Swift's fifth album, *1989*, is released on October 27 and sells 1.287 million copies during its first week on the market. Swift is named the 2014 Woman of the Year by Billboard.

In January, *Fearless* wins Album of the Year at the Grammys; in February, *Valentine's Day* hits the big screen; Swift's third album *Speak Now* hits store shelves on October 24, selling over one million copies in its first week.

On November 27, *1989* celebrates one year in the Billboard's Top Ten.

2015

Swift is presented with the Pinnacle Award at the CMAs.

2010

2013

SOURCE NOTES

Chapter One

Page 6: Quoted by Vanessa Grigoriadis, "The Very Pink, Very Perfect Life of Taylor Swift," March 5, 2009, www.rollingstone.com/music/news/the-very-pink-very-perfect-life-of-taylor-swift-20090305#ixzz3xYnC76DR.

Page 8: "Katie's Couric's 'All Access' Grammy Special: Taylor Swift," *CBS News,* January 30, 2009, www.cbsnews.com/videos/all-access-taylor-swift.

Page 9: Quoted by Josh Eells, "22 Things You Learn Hanging Out with Taylor Swift," *Rolling Stone,* September 10, 2014, www.rolling-stone.com/music/news/22-things-you-learn-hanging-out-with-taylor-swift-20140910.

Page 11: Quoted by Craig Mclean, "Taylor Swift: 'Maybe I should just lighten up,'" *The Independent*, October 23, 2010. www.independent.co.uk/arts-entertainment/music/features/taylor-swift-maybe-i-should-just-lighten-up-2112052.html.

Page 12: Quoted by Don Botch, "Taylor Swift superstar: How pop's biggest singer began her career in Berks," *Reading Eagle*, December 7, 2014, www.readingeagle.com/news/article/taylor-swift-superstar#sthash.UyOaiF5j.dpuf.

Page 13: Swift, *Taylor Swift: Journey to Fearless*.

Page 14: Jepson, Louisa, *Taylor Swift,* (New York, NY: Simon and Schuster, 2013) p.22.

Page 16: "Behind the song, a list of Taylor's story behind some of her songs," http://www.fanpop.com/clubs/taylor-swift/articles/34352/title/behind-song-list-taylors-story-behind-some-songs.

Page 18: Quoted by Shelly Akers, "Taylor Swift Reveals 'I'm Kind of a Neat Freak," *People*, June 9, 2008, www.people.com/people/article/0,,20205142,00.html

Chapter Two

Page 22: Quoted by Jon Caramanica, "My Music, MySpace, My Life," *New York Times*. November 8, 2008, www.nytimes.com/2008/11/09/arts/music/09cara.html?_r=1&pagewanted=all.

Page 23: Quoted by John Preston, "Taylor Swift: the 19-year-old country music star conquering America - and now Britain*,"* *The Telegraph*, April 26, 2009. www.telegraph.co.uk/culture/music/rockandpopmusic/5202294/Taylor-Swift-the-19-year-old-country-music-star-conquering-America-and-now-Britain.html.

Page 23: Quoted by Ed McGraw, "When She Thinks 'Tim McGraw,' Taylor Swift Savors Payoff," *CMT*, December 1, 2006, www.cmt.com/news/1546980/when-she-thinks-tim-mcgraw-taylor-swift-savors-payoff.

Page 26: Swift, Taylor, "Tim McGraw," by Taylor Swift and Liz Rose, in *Taylor Swift*. Big Machine, 2006, http://taylorswift.com/releases#/release/2812.

Page 29: Quoted by Caramanica, "My Music, MySpace, My Life."

Page 29: Quoted by McGraw. "When She Thinks 'Tim McGraw,' Taylor Swift Savors Payoff."

Page 31: *"Taylor Swift* track list," http://taylorswift.com/releases#/release/2812.

Page 32: Quoted by Deborah Evans-Price, "Memorable CMA Awards Acceptance Speeches," *The Boot*, November 9, 2010, http://theboot.com/cma-awards-acceptance-speeches/?trackback=tsmclip.

Chapter Three

Page 33-34: Quoted by Andrew Lahey, "Songwriter Spotlight: Liz Rose," *Rolling Stone*, October 24, 2014, www.rollingstone.com/music/albumreviews/fearless-20081113.

Page 37: Swift, Taylor, *"Fearless: The Platinum Edition* track list," http://taylorswift.com/releases#/release/2822.

Page 40: Rosen, Judy, "Review of *Fearless,"Rolling Stone*. November 13, 2008, www.rollingstone.com/music/albumreviews/fearless-20081113.

Page 41: Swift, *Taylor Swift: Journey to Fearless.*

Page 41: Swift, Taylor, "'Best Day' lyrics," http://taylorswift.com/releases#/release/2822.

Page 45: Quoted by Daniel Kreps, "Kanye West Storms the VMAs Stage During Taylor Swift's Speech," *Rolling Stone*, September 13, 2009, www.rollingstone.com/music/news/kanye-west-storms-the-vmas-stage-during-taylor-swifts-speech-20090913.

Page 46: Swift, Taylor, "'Innocent' lyrics," http://taylorswift.com/releases#/release/2832.

Page 46: Quoted by Erin Strecker, "Kanye West & Taylor Swift: A Complete Timeline of Their Relationship," *Billboard*, September 8, 2015, www.billboard.com/articles/news/6686064/kanye-west-taylor-swift-relationship-timeline.

Page 47: "Taylor Swift, Your Label Chief Defends Your Grammy Performance…Although You Weren't Perfect, You 'Had Heart,'" *Hollywood Life*, February 4, 2010, http://hollywoodlife.com/2010/02/04/taylor-swift-grammy-performance-sucked-says-label-chief.

Chapter Four

Page 52: Quoted by Tom Roland, "Taylor Swift ready to 'Speak Now' with third album," *Reuters,* October 15, 2010, www.reuters.com/article/us-swift-idUSTRE69E5RK20101015?pageNumber=3.

Page 53: Quoted by Jocelyn Vena, "Taylor Swift *Red* with Emotion on New Album," *MTV News*, September 4, 2012, www.mtv.com/news/1693123/taylor-swift-red-new-album.

Page 53: Simon, Carly. "'You're So Vain' lyrics," www.azlyrics.com/lyrics/carlysimon/youresovain.html.

Pg. 54: Swift, Taylor. "*Red: The Deluxe Edition* track list," http://taylor-swift.com/releases#/release/7301.

Page 55: Swift, Taylor, *Twitter,* https://twitter.com/taylorswift13/status/361344042333773824.

Page 55: Quoted by Elio Iannacci, "Carly Simon on Mick Jagger, Taylor Swift—and being herself," *Maclean's*, January 3, 2016, www.macleans.ca/culture/arts/carly-simon-on-mick-jagger-taylor-swift-and-being-herself.

Page 55: Quoted by Josh Eells, "The Reinvention of Taylor Swift," *Rolling Stone*, September 8, 2014, www.rollingstone.com/music/features/taylor-swift-1989-cover-story-20140908.

Page 56: Quoted by Ray Rogers, "Taylor Swift: Billboard Music Award Wins Were a 'Wonderful Feeling,'" *Billboard*, May 25, 2013, www.billboard.com/articles/events/bbma-2013/1563860/taylor-swift-billboard-music-award-wins-were-a-wonderful-feeling.

Page 59: Jamik, Jaelyn, "Taylor Swift congratulated for CMA Pinnacle Award by celebrity line up," Examiner, November 7, 2013, www.examiner.com/article/taylor-swift-congratulated-for-cma-pinnacle-award-by-celebrity-line-up.

Chapter Five

Page 64: Ganz, Caryn et al, "MTV VMAs 2014's 20 Best and Worst Moments," *Rolling Stone*, November 16, 2014, www.rollingstone. com/music/lists/mtv-vmas-2014s-20-best-and-worst-moments-20140825#ixzz3xHVNBg00.

Page 64: Quoted by Daniel Kreps, "Taylor Swift Dismisses the Haters, Dances With Fans for New Song 'Shake it Off,'" *Rolling Stone*, August 18, 2014, www.rollingstone.com/music/news/taylor-swift-dismisses-the-haters-dances-with-fans-for-new-song-shake-it-off.

Page 65: Quoted by Chuck Klosterman, "Taylor Swift on 'Bad Blood,' Kanye West, and How People Interpret her Lyrics," *GQ*, October 15, 2015, www.gq.com/story/taylor-swift-gq-cover-story.

Page 65: Quoted by Sophie Schillaci, "EXCLUSIVE: Taylor Swift on Best Friends, Boyfriends and Blurring the Lines Between Pop and Country," *ET Online*, October 27, 2014, www.etonline.com/music/153022_taylor_swift_1989_best_friends_boyfriends_blurring_lines_pop_country.

Pg. 69: Swift, Taylor, "1989 Track List," http://taylorswift.com/releases#/release/12453.

Page 72: Quoted by David Browne, "Ryan Adams on His Full-Album Taylor Swift Cover: 'You Just Have to Mean It,'" *Rolling Stone*, September 21, 2015, www. rollingstone.com/music/news/ryan-adams-on-his-full-album-taylor-swift-cover-you-just-have-to-mean-it-20150921.

Page 72: Swift, Twitter, https://twitter.com/taylorswift13/status/644535114203025408?lang=en.

Page 72: Dunham, Lena, Twitter, https://twitter.com/lenadunham/status/644879576015966208?ref_src=twsrc%5Etfw.

Page 74: Lowe, Zane, "Beats 1 Interview with Taylor Swift," https://itunes.apple.com/us/post/idsa.32246a32-a20d-11e5-ac2e-6c56662bf630.

Page 77: Preuss, Andrea, Chris Isidore and Samuel Burke, "Taylor Swift shakes, shakes, shakes off copyright lawsuit," CNN, November 12, 2015, www.cnn.com/2015/11/12/us/taylor-swift-copyright-lawsuit-dismissed.

Chapter Six

Page 81: Quoted by Eileen Finan, "Taylor Swift Helps Raise Millions for Nashville Flood Relief," *People*, May 7, 2010, www.people.com/people/article/0,,20367527,00.htmlMother cancer

Page 84: Swift, Taylor, "Just So You Know," http://taylorswift.tumblr.com/post/115942142045/just-so-you-know

Page 85: Swift, Taylor, "World of Tay Swift," http://taylorswift.tumblr.com/post/109275791245/worldoftayswift-worldoftayswift

Page 88: Swift, Taylor, "For Taylor Swift, the Future of Music Is a Love Story," *Wall Street Journal*, July 7, 2014, www.wsj.com/articles/for-taylor-swift-the-future-of-music-is-a-love-story-1404763219

Page 90: Quoted by Alan Light, "Billboard Woman of the Year Taylor Swift on Writing Her Own Rules, Not Becoming a Cliche and the Hurdle of Going Pop," *Billboard*, December 5, 2014, http://www.billboard.com/articles/events/women-in-music-2014/6363514/billboard-woman-of-the-year-taylor-swift-on-writing-her

Page 91: Swift, Taylor, "To Apple, Love Taylor," http://taylorswift.tumblr.com/post/122071902085/to-apple-love-taylor

Page 92-93: Quoted by Mark Sutherland, "Taylor Swift inteview: 'A relationship? No one's going to sign up for this,'" *Telegraph*, May 23, 2015, www.telegraph.co.uk/culture/music/rockandpopfeatures/11430433/Taylor-Swift-interview-A-relationship-No-ones-going-to-sign-up-for-this.html

Page 93: Quoted by Josh Duboff, "Taylor Swift: Apple Crusader, #GirlSquad Captain, and the Most Influential 25-Year-Old in America," *Vanity Fair*, August 31, 2015. /www.vanityfair.com/style/2015/08/taylor-swift-cover-mario-testino-apple-music

Page 93: Swift, "For Taylor Swift, the Future of Music Is a Love Story."

GLOSSARY

cover A new performance of a song that has been previously recorded or performed by another artist.

crossover In music, achieving success by moving from one genre to another, such as from country to pop.

demo A recording that showcases a prospective artist's talent.

development deal A first agreement between a record company and an artist to develop the artist's talent in lieu of royalties.

endorse To publicly represent a product or service.

extended play (EP) A short album which is not as long as a full-length record.

gold A certification awarded when an album sells five hundred thousand copies.

headlining Being featured as the main artist on a tour.

honky-tonk A kind of lively music, usually played on the piano, with a distinctive, heavy beat.

indie Independent; typically used to describe a film or music production company.

platinum A certification given to a single or album that sells more than one million copies.

showcase A performance showing off an artist's skills.

FURTHER INFORMATION

Books

Newkey-Burden, Chase. *Taylor Swift: The Whole Story*. New York: HarperCollins, 2014.

Parker, Jill. *TAY: The Taylor Swift Story*. Beverly Hills, CA: Sole Books, 2015.

Spencer, Liv. *Taylor Swift: The Platinum Edition*. Toronto, Canada: ECW Press, 2013.

Websites

AMEX: Taylor Swift Unstaged

www.americanexpress.com/us/content/unstaged-app/index.html

Explore the world of Swift's single "Blank Space" through this free interactive app by American Express, available through the Apple App Store or Google Play.

Billboard.com: Taylor Swift

www.billboard.com/artist/371422/taylor-swift

The Billboard website gives up-to-date information on Swift's latest hits and also includes her biography and links to videos, articles, and photos.

Grammy Pro: Listening Session With
Taylor Swift: *1989*

www.grammypro.com/professional-development/video/listening-session-taylor-swift-1989-part-1

In this three-part interview, Swift explains her songwriting process and growth as an artist that led to her recordbreaking *1989* album.

NME: Taylor Swift's Extraordinary Career In Numbers Infographic

www.nme.com/blogs/the-big-picture/taylor-swifts-extraordinary-career-in-numbers-infographic

This infographic breaks down some of Swift's career highlights and provides readers with some fun trivia.

People: Taylor Swift Timeline

www.people.com/people/taylor_swift/biography/0,,20179014,00.html

This website includes a detailed timeline of Swift's journey to the top.

Tumblr: Taylor Swift

taylorswift.tumblr.com

Follow Swift on Tumblr for the latest updates from the star herself.

Films

Speak Now World Tour Live, DVD, 2011

Taylor Swift: Journey to Fearless, DVD, 2010

Taylor Swift: The 1989 World Tour Live, available via Apple Music, 2015

Up Front: Taylor Swift, DVD, 2014

BIBLIOGRAPHY

Browne, David. "Ryan Adams on His Full-Album Taylor Swift Cover: 'You Just Have to Mean It'" *Rolling Stone*. September 21, 2015. Accessed January 11, 2016. www.rollingstone.com/music/news/ryan-adams-on-his-full-album-taylor-swift-cover-you-just-have-to-mean-it-20150921.

Caulfield, Keith. "Both Taylor Swift and Ryan Adams' '1989' Albums Are in Top 10 of Billboard 200 Chart." *Billboard*. September 27, 2015. Accessed January 11, 2016. www.billboard.com/articles/columns/chart-beat/6708141/taylor-swift-ryan-adams-1989-albums-top-10.

Cupp, Tonya Maddox. *Taylor Swift*. New York: Cavendish Square Publishing, 2015.

Donnelly, Erin. "Taylor Swift Just Made a HUGE Charity Move." Refinery 29. July 12, 2015. www.refinery29.com/2015/07/90590/taylor-swift-gofundme-charity-donation

Eells, Josh. "The Reinvention of Taylor Swift." *Rolling Stone*. September 8, 2014. Accessed December 30, 2015. www.rollingstone.com/music/features/taylor-swift-1989-cover-story-20140908.

Eells, Josh. "22 Things You Learn Hanging Out With Taylor Swift." *Rolling Stone*. September 10, 2014. www.rollingstone.com/music/news/22-things-you-learn-hanging-out-with-taylor-swift-20140910.

Iannacci, Elio. "Carly Simon on Mick Jagger, Taylor Swift—and being herself." *Maclean's*. January 3, 2016. Accessed January 6, 2016. www.macleans.ca/culture/arts/carly-simon-on-mick-jagger-taylor-swift-and-being-herself.

"Katie Couric's 'All Access' Grammy Special: Taylor Swift" CBS News. January 30, 2009. www.cbsnews.com/videos/all-access-taylor-swift.

Klosterman, Chuck. "Taylor Swift on 'Bad Blood,' Kanye West, and How People Interpret her Lyrics." *GQ*. October 15, 2015. Accessed December 26, 2015. www.gq.com/story/taylor-swift-gq-cover-story.

Kreps, Daniel. "Kanye West Storms the VMAs Stage During Taylor Swift's Speech." *Rolling Stone*. September 13, 2009. Accessed January 4, 2016. www.rollingstone.com/music/news/kanye-west-storms-the-vmas-stage-during-taylor-swifts-speech-20090913.

Lipshutz, Jason. "Taylor Swift's 'Blank Space' App: Inside the User Experience." *Billboard*. November 11, 2014. www.billboard.com/articles/columns/pop-shop/6312276/taylor-swift-blank-space-app.

Malec, Jim. "Taylor Swift: The Garden in the Machine." *American Songwriter*. May 2, 2011. Accessed December 30, 2015. http://americansongwriter.com/2011/05/taylor-swift-the-garden-in-the-machine.

Mclean, Craig. "Taylor Swift: 'Maybe I should just lighten up'." *The Independent*. October 23, 2010. Accessed January 8, 2016. www.independent.co.uk/arts-entertainment/music/features/taylor-swift-maybe-i-should-just-lighten-up-2112052.html.

Norwin, Alyssa. "Taylor Swift Chokes Up In Concert Talking About Her Mother's Battle With Cancer." *Hollywood Life*. August 18, 2015. Accessed January 7, 2016. http://hollywoodlife.com/2015/08/18/taylor-swift-mom-cancer-cries-ronan-arizona-concert.

Rogers, Alex. "Q&A: Why Taylor Swift Thinks Nashville Is the Best Place on Earth. *Time*. March 7, 2014. Accessed December 30, 2015. time.com/14933/taylor-swift-nashville-interview.

"Songwriter Taylor Swift Signs Publishing Deal with Sony/ATV." BMI. May 12, 2005. www.bmi.com/news/entry/20050512Taylor_Swift_Songwriter_Taylor_Swift_Signs_Publishing_Deal_With.

Spencer, Liv. *Taylor Swift: The Platinum Edition*. Toronto, Canada: ECW Press, 2013.

Strecker, Erin. "10 Taylor Swift Good Deeds That Warmed Our Hearts." *Billboard*. July 13, 2015. Accessed December 30, 2015. www.billboard.com/articles/events/fan-army/6620410/taylor-swift-good-deeds-fans.

Strecker, Erin. "Watch Taylor Swift's Amazing 'Blank Space' Performance at Grammy Museum." *Billboard*. January 7, 2016. Accessed January 7, 2016. www.billboard.com/articles/columns/pop/6836066/taylor-swift-blank-space-performance-grammy-museum.

Stubbs, Dan. "Taylor Swift: Power, Fame And The Future." *NME*. October 9, 2015. Accessed January 7, 2016. www.nme.com/features/taylor-swift-power-fame-and-the-future-the-full-nme-cover-interview.

Takeda, Allison. "Taylor Swift Gets Choked Up Talking About Cancer, Gives Rare Performance of "Ronan."" *US Magazine*. August 18, 2015. Accessed January 14, 2016. www.usmagazine.com/celebrity-news/news/taylor-swift-tears-up-talking-about-cancer-performs-ronan-2015188.

"Taylor Swift Interview." *The Stacks*. January 25, 2013. Accessed January 4, 2016. http://blog.scholastic.com/ink_splot_26/taylor-swift-interview.html.

"Taylor Swift: Speak Now—Treasures from the World Tour." Country Music Hall of Fame and Museum. countrymusichalloffame.org/exhibits/exhibitdetail/taylor-swift-speak-nowtreasures-from-the-world-tour.

"Taylor Swift to Receive CMA Pinnacle Award at 2013 CMA Awards." CMA World. November 4, 2013. www.cmaworld.com/cma-awards/2013/11/04/taylor-swift-receive-cma-pinnacle-award-2013-cma-awards.

Testino, Mario. "Taylor Swift: Apple Crusader, #GirlSquad Captain, and the Most Influential 25-Year-Old in America." *Vanity Fair*. August 31, 2015. www.vanityfair.com/style/2015/08/taylor-swift-cover-mario-testino-apple-music.

Thompson, Gayle. "Taylor Swift Takes Time to Reflect on Her Success." *The Boot.* February 4, 2010. http://theboot.com/taylor-swift-grammy-awards.

Vaughan, Andrew. *Taylor Swift*. New York: Sterling Publishing, 2011.

Widdicombe, Lizzie. "You Belong with Me." *New Yorker*. October 10, 2011. Accessed December 26, 2015. www.newyorker.com/magazine/2011/10/10/you-belong-with-me.

Willman, Chris. "Big Machine's Scott Borchetta on Taylor Swift, the Fight Against Free and Remaining 'Bold and Disruptive' on 10-Year Anniversary." *Billboard*. October 26, 2015. Accessed January 7, 2016. www.billboard.com/articles/business/6738578/scott-borchetta-big-machine-10-year-anniversary-interview.

Willman, Chris. "Getting to know Taylor Swift." *Entertainment Weekly*. July 25, 2007. Accessed December 30, 2015. www.ew.com/article/2007/07/25/getting-know-taylor-swift.

Yahr, Emily. "How Taylor Swift really, truly said goodbye to country music at the ACM Awards." *Washington Post*. April 20, 2015. Accessed December 30, 2015. www.washingtonpost.com/news/arts-and-entertainment/wp/2015/04/20/how-taylor-swift-really-truly-said-goodbye-to-country-music-at-the-acm-awards.

INDEX

Page numbers in **boldface** are illustrations. Entries in **boldface** are glossary terms.

ABOUT THE AUTHOR

Kelly Spence works as a freelance author and editor for educational publishers and holds a BA in English and Liberal Arts from Brock University. She also earned a Certificate in Publishing from Ryerson University. When she's not buried in a book, Kelly is busy cooking with her husband or playing with her lovable boxer, Zoey. Kelly has been a longtime fan of Taylor Swift, from her early days singing country to her new pop material. Her current favorite Swift song is a toss-up between "Shake It Off" and "Wildest Dreams."